D0899051

MONUMENTAL MILESTONES
GREAT EVENTS OF MODERN TIMES

The Sinking of the *Titanic*

DISCARD

When she began service in 1912, the *Titanic* was the world's largest passenger ship.

Mitchell Lane
PUBLISHERS

P.O. Box 196
Hockessin, Delaware 19707

Titles in the Series

MONUMENTAL MILESTONES
GREAT EVENTS OF MODERN TIMES

The Sinking of the *Titanic*

A 1985 photo shows part of the wreckage of the *Titanic*.

Jim Whiting

Copyright © 2007 by Mitchell Lane Publishers, Inc. All rights reserved. No part of this book may be reproduced without written permission from the publisher. Printed and bound in the United States of America.

Printing   2   3   4   5   6   7   8   9

Library of Congress Cataloging-in-Publication Data
Whiting, Jim, 1943–
   The sinking of the Titanic / by Jim Whiting.
      p. cm. — (Monumental milestones)
   Includes bibliographical references and index.
   ISBN 1-58415-472-1 (library bound : alk. paper)
   1. Titanic (Steamship)—Juvenile literature. 2. Shipwrecks—North Atlantic Ocean—Juvenile literature. I. Title. II. Series.
   G530.T6W53 2006
   910.9163'4—dc22
                                                                                  2005036805

ISBN-10: 1-58415-472-1   ISBN-13: 978-1-58415-472-3

ABOUT THE AUTHOR: Jim Whiting has been a remarkably versatile and accomplished journalist, writer, editor, and photographer for more than 30 years. A voracious reader since early childhood, Mr. Whiting has written and edited about 200 nonfiction children's books. His subjects range from authors to zoologists and include contemporary pop icons and classical musicians, saints and scientists, emperors and explorers. Representative titles include *The Life and Times of Franz Liszt*, *The Life and Times of Julius Caesar*, *Charles Schulz*, *Charles Darwin and the Origin of the Species*, *Juan Ponce de Leon*, and *The Scopes Monkey Trial*.

    Other career highlights are a lengthy stint publishing *Northwest Runner*, the first piece of original fiction to appear in *Runners World* magazine, hundreds of descriptions and venue photographs for America Online, e-commerce product writing, sports editor for the *Bainbridge Island Review*, light verse in a number of magazines, and acting as the official photographer for the Antarctica Marathon.

    He lives in Washington State with his wife and two teenage sons.

PHOTO CREDITS: Cover—Superstock; p. 1—GB Marine Art; pp. 3, 34, 41—Emory Kristof/National Geographic/NOAA; pp. 6, 20—Time Life Pictures/Getty Images; pp. 8, 26, 32—Hulton Archive/Getty Images; pp. 11, 14, 31—Topical Press Agency/Getty Images; p. 17—Science Museum; p. 18—Navy History; p. 23—Institut für Informatik; p. 38—*The Rocky Mountain News*.

PLB2,4

Contents

The Sinking of the *Titanic*

Jim Whiting

*For Your Information

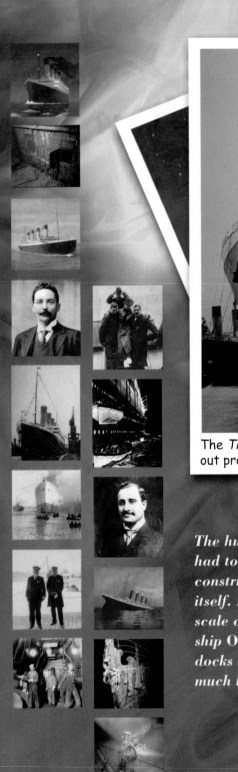

The *Titanic* undergoes the final stages of the fitting-out process.

The huge crane on the dock had to be specially constructed. So did the dock itself. Because of the massive scale of Titanic and her sister ship Olympic, three original docks were made into two much larger ones.

Built to Be Unsinkable

On a warm summer evening in 1907, J. Bruce Ismay and his wife enjoyed an excellent dinner. They were guests at the luxurious London home of Lord and Lady William Pirrie. When the servants cleared away the dessert dishes, Ismay and Pirrie excused themselves from their wives. It was time to talk business. The two men retreated to Pirrie's smoking room. They sipped coffee and smoked expensive cigars.

Ismay was chairman of the White Star Line, one of the world's largest and most important passenger steamship companies. Pirrie headed Harland and Wolff shipyard, located in Belfast, Ireland (now Northern Ireland). White Star was the yard's most important customer.

White Star was one of several companies in the lucrative transatlantic passenger business. The competition was ferocious. Many people focused on winning the Blue Riband, the award for the fastest crossing.

The Cunard Line, another British company, had just launched two new ships, *Lusitania* and the *Mauretania*. They were designed to be very fast. These new ships generated a great deal of favorable publicity for Cunard. They cut into the number of passengers that White Star was carrying.

That was why Ismay and Pirrie were meeting on that June evening. They needed to do something to put White Star back into the headlines. The two men quickly realized that they were on the same page. They had no interest in the Blue Riband. White Star stood for something else. As maritime writers Tom McCluskie, Michael Sharpe, and Leo Marriott observe, "Although the [White Star] vessels may be slower than their rivals, they were outfitted to the highest standard of craftsmanship using only the very best materials and equipment available. In short, White Star epitomized

J. Bruce Ismay joined the White Star Line when he was just a teenager.

Ismay's father, Thomas Ismay, bought the White Star Line, one of the world's largest steamship companies, in 1868. Bruce eventually became director and chairman of the company.

the very finest in elegance and style . . . they would leave the vulgar pursuit of speed to others."[1]

As a result, both men were "thinking big." Literally. They wanted to build the world's largest passenger liners. In an era in which "bigger" meant "better," they knew the news would generate tremendous interest. These liners would add to White Star's reputation for luxury, yet they also had to be reasonably fast. Many travelers were businessmen who couldn't afford to spend too much time at sea.

Ismay and Pirrie decided to build three ships. They wanted to establish a system of regular, reliable weekly crossings. It would be too much of a strain on two ships. Three would be just right.

They quickly sketched the outlines of the ships. They would be nearly 900 feet long and weigh well over 40,000 tons. Those dimensions were far larger than any other ships. To drive the point home, White Star issued advertisements. These ads showed how the ships would compare with famous manmade structures if they were stood on their ends. Far higher than the Washington Monument. Nearly double the height of the Great Pyramid at Giza, Egypt, which had been earth's highest structure for 4,300 years. Nearly 150 feet higher than New York's Woolworth Building, which was then under construction and would be the world's tallest building.

Ismay and Pirrie turned their rough sketches over to the designers at Harland and Wolff. The designers went to work. In 1908, their designs were approved.

The ships' statistics were staggering. Each one needed more than 24,000 tons of steel. Three million rivets (which weighed a ton and a half) held all the steel together. Two of the ship's three propellers stood 23 feet high. The third was 16 feet. Their combined weight was nearly 100 tons. Their three anchors weighed about 10 tons apiece. One hundred fifty-nine furnaces gulped more than 800 tons of coal each day. These furnaces provided heat for 29 boilers. Each ship loomed 175 feet up from the keel to the top of the four smokestacks. The stacks were 62 feet high. They were wide enough to accommodate two sets of railroad tracks.

In reality, the ships needed only three smokestacks, but the largest and most prestigious ships in other lines had four. Many travelers also believed that more smokestacks indicated a safer ship. Harland and Wolff's designers added a fourth smokestack. It was a dummy. No smoke would ever pass through it.

Media hype guaranteed that many people would be aware of this avalanche of numbers. One number, however, went almost unnoticed.

It was twenty.

That was the number of lifeboats the vessels would carry. Fully loaded, these twenty lifeboats would hold just under 1,200 people. Yet the ships were designed to contain nearly 3,500 passengers and crew members.

There were two reasons for what seems to be a tragic oversight. One was that the lifeboat capacity was actually well over the legal minimum. According to British shipping regulations, the lifeboats needed to accommodate only 962 people. These regulations had been drawn up more than twenty years previously by the British Board of Trade. At that time, a ship of more than 10,000 tons was a rarity. Twenty lifeboats were more than enough for a ship of that size. No one had bothered to update the regulations in the explosion of size and passenger accommodation that had occurred since then.

The other reason was the actual purpose of the lifeboats. No one seriously believed that these huge ships could founder. Fifteen watertight doors divided them into sixteen compartments. The designers believed the ships would remain afloat indefinitely even if several compartments were flooded. There would be plenty of time for rescue ships to arrive. Basically, the big ships would serve as their own lifeboats.

The lifeboats onboard would be used to transport passengers and crewmen from the stricken vessel to nearby rescue ships. No one seriously believed that the ships would ever need the lifeboats. Nor could they anticipate any situation in which other ships wouldn't be close by. The North Atlantic shipping lanes always had a lot of traffic.

The plans that Ismay and Pirrie drew up were grandiose, as were the names they chose. These names reflected their education. Most British leaders at that time studied ancient Greek classics in school. Ismay and Pirrie thought that giving their ships names that came from the Greeks would add to their importance. One name was *Gigantic*. It is the origin of the word *giant*. Another was *Olympic*. It came from Mount Olympus, the name of the home of the ancient gods of Greece. The third came from an even older and much larger group of mythical beings. It was *Titanic*.

Plans called for *Olympic* and *Titanic* to be built almost simultaneously. Then *Gigantic* would follow.

Construction began on *Olympic* on December 16, 1908. Work on *Titanic* got under way on March 31 the following year. *Olympic* was launched on October 20, 1910. The huge vessel needed more than seven months to be completely fitted out. She finally left Belfast on May 31, 1911. To add to the festivities, Harland and Wolff launched *Titanic* the same day. The twin events attracted many thousands of onlookers.

Passengers packed *Olympic* on her maiden voyage, which began on June 14, 1911. She crossed without any problems. After several additional crossings, Ismay decided to make some changes in *Titanic*. Most were cen-

Olympic's maiden voyage began June 14, 1911. Unlike her unfortunate sister, the Titanic, *the* Olympic *made many transatlantic crossings.*

The *Olympic* (above) was virtually identical to the *Titanic*.

tered on ways of making more money. Public areas were reduced. More cabins for big spenders were built.

As a result, *Titanic* became nine inches longer and a few hundred tons heavier than her sister. She was now the largest ship in the world.

Media interest in the big ships hadn't stopped when *Olympic* went into service. If anything, it was even greater. As *Titanic*'s completion date approached, a maritime magazine gushed, "The Captain may, by simply moving an electric switch, instantly close the doors throughout and make the vessel practically unsinkable."[2]

Other media picked up the "practically unsinkable" refrain. It wasn't too long before the refrain lost the qualifying "practically."

Titanic became—at least in the public mind—unsinkable. Even more than *Olympic*, she seemed to represent the ultimate in man's superiority over the natural world. As a U.S. Senate investigation would later acknowledge, "Mastery of the ocean had at last been achieved."[3]

The builders were fully aware of the Greek roots of the ship's names. They probably didn't consider another Greek idea. That was the concept of hubris. *Hubris* means "pride." The Greeks wrote many tragic plays, a great number of which were centered on the consequences of hubris. Because of his *hubris*, the hero was brought down.

The Greeks believed that seeing the effects of hubris would serve as a warning to their spectators. Act in this way, the playwrights appeared to be saying, and you too will suffer the same fate.

It wasn't just the Greeks who recognized the pitfalls of pride. Several centuries earlier, the Hebrew King Solomon had become the principal writer of the Book of Proverbs. One of the proverbs, in retrospect, was applicable to the story of *Titanic*: "Pride goeth before destruction, and an haughty spirit before a fall."[4]

As the final touches were being made to *Titanic* early in 1912, Mother Nature was apparently preparing her response to this display of pride.

Every year, huge chunks of ice break off from glaciers in Greenland and other Arctic regions. The larger chunks become icebergs. They can be more than 200 feet high and weigh many tons. Most of an iceberg lies below the surface. That can make icebergs hard to see at night. Other times the chunks fragment into smaller pieces that remain close together. This is called pack ice. Sometimes pack ice can stretch for dozens of miles.

The winter of 1911–1912 had been unusually mild. As a result, even more ice broke off than usual. Thousands of icebergs and fields of pack ice slowly began drifting south. Eventually they drifted into the path of the hundreds of ships that crisscrossed the North Atlantic Ocean.

The *Hawke*

Olympic's first few voyages bore out her builders' optimism. The ship received rave reviews from her passengers. Then she suffered two mishaps. On September 20, 1911, she was involved in a collision with the British warship *Hawke*. Despite two flooded compartments, *Olympic* remained afloat. That added credence to the "unsinkable" myth. The following February she lost a propeller blade. She made another trip back to the shipyard after *Titanic's* loss to undergo a number of safety modifications.

When World War I broke out in 1914, *Olympic* became a troop carrier. Her speed allowed her to outrun German U-boats. Once she turned the tables on the enemy. She surprised a U-boat on the surface early in 1918. Incredibly, the submarine's lookouts didn't see the massive ship bearing down on them. Before the submarine could dive, *Olympic* sliced through it.

During the 1920s, *Olympic* made many voyages across the Atlantic. The Great Depression, which began in 1929, cut back the number of passengers who could afford the trip. *Olympic*, like other ships, was affected. Her size made her very expensive to operate.

In 1935 she was sold for scrap. It required nearly two years to cut the huge ship apart. Most of the steel was recycled for use in World War II British warships.

Gigantic's keel was laid down in 1911. After the *Titanic* disaster, her name was changed to *Britannic*. Like *Olympic*, she had several new safety features. It was then estimated that she could survive with six compartments flooded.

The *Olympic*

The British government decided to use *Britannic* as a hospital ship. She made a number of trips back and forth between the Mediterranean and England, carrying wounded soldiers. Late in 1916, she was en route to pick up another load of casualties. She struck a mine off the Greek coast. Not all the watertight doors could be shut. Water poured in through open portholes. The captain tried to beach the ship on a nearby island. That forced even more water into the ship. *Britannic* sank in less than an hour. Nearly all of the 1,000 crewmen and hospital personnel were saved.

Lord William Pirrie (left) and Captain Edward J. Smith stand aboard the *Olympic*.

Pirrie was a director of Harland and Wolff, the company that built the Titanic. Smith went to sea at the age of 17. He commanded ships for nearly 40 years, until he went down with Titanic.

The Maiden Voyage Begins

Olympic had two serious accidents as she continued to operate. Both times she returned to Harland and Wolff for repairs. Both times she diverted men and equipment from *Titanic*. *Titanic*'s original sailing date of March 20, 1912, had to be postponed. It was rescheduled for April 10.

The postponement reflected badly on White Star. The company was under a lot of pressure to avoid further delays. When work on *Titanic* was finally completed, she put out from Belfast harbor on April 2 for her sea trials. The trials took only a few hours. It was nowhere near enough time for the officers to become familiar with the way the ship handled.

Then she departed for Southampton, a major port on the southern coast of England. There were many preparations to complete in a short period of time. The vessel had to take on coal and provisions. Most of the crew members had to be hired. Nearly 600 tons of cargo had to be loaded and stowed in the three forward holds.

The feverish work continued into the morning of April 10. The crew held a brief lifeboat drill. They were not assigned to specific stations. Soon afterward, the passengers began arriving.

The early 1900s was an era that worshiped wealth. Many rich people were on board. Perhaps the most noted—certainly the most notorious—was John Jacob Astor IV. His great-grandfather had been one of the pioneers in the lucrative fur trade in the West. The town of Astoria, Oregon, was named for him. John Jacob Astor IV, now forty-seven, had recently gone through a messy and widely publicized divorce. He married Madeleine Talmadge on the rebound. She was eighteen, and she was pregnant.

Benjamin Guggenheim was another rich passenger. He had made a fortune in mining. Isidor Straus owned Macy's, at that time the world's largest department store. George Widener had made his money in building railroad cars and urban streetcars.

Not all the "big-bucks" passengers were men. Margaret "Maggie" Brown of Colorado was famous in her home state. She was active in charity work. She made good use of the wealth that her husband's gold mining work had created.

Of course, not everyone on board *Titanic* was wealthy. The ship carried more than 700 people in third class. Even their accommodations were better than those on most other ships. Theirs was a far cry from the situation that had existed barely two decades earlier. Then, many of the ships carrying people to America transported livestock when they returned. There often wasn't enough time for cleaning between voyages.

Different accounts give slightly different figures for the number of people on board *Titanic* on her maiden voyage. The figures include about 330 in first class, 290 in second class, and the 700-plus in third class. The total was only about half her capacity. One of the main reasons was a coal strike in England, which created a serious disruption of travel schedules.

A handful of passengers may have been aware of an 1898 book called *Futility* by Morgan Robertson. The storyline was about a huge steamer named *Titan*. The ship struck an iceberg in April and sank with heavy loss of life. According to Robertson, the vessel represented the height of luxury. It was "the largest craft afloat and the greatest of the works of men."[1] *Titan* carried 24 lifeboats, very close to *Titanic*'s 20. The lack of lifeboats didn't matter because of the ship's "nineteen water-tight compartments. . . . With nine compartments flooded the ship would still float, and as no known incident of the sea could possibly fill this many, the steamship *Titan* was considered practically unsinkable."[2]

There were also about 900 crew members. Some were very visible to the passengers, such as the ship's officers and the stewards and waiters in the dining rooms. Others were invisible. These were people such as the stokers. They had a very filthy and uncomfortable job. They had to constantly shovel coal into the ship's furnaces. White Star wanted to make sure

The first-class cabins were much more expensive than second-class and third-class accommodations. When it came to meals, first-class passengers even had separate menus from which to order.

These first-class cabins were designed to be the last word in shipboard luxury.

that the passengers never saw men like these. They slept in the bow of the ship. When it was time to go to work, they went aft through a special passageway.

In charge of these approximately 2,220 people was Captain Edward J. Smith. He looked the perfect part of the sea captain, with his carefully trimmed white beard and weathered features. At the age of sixty-two, he had been at sea for most of his life. He had planned on making *Titanic*'s first voyage his last. It was—but not in the way he had intended.

Smith took his ship out of her berth in Southampton shortly after noon on April 10. *Titanic* began to pass the steamer *New York*, which was tied up at a nearby pier. The tremendous suction generated by *Titanic*'s propellers snapped *New York*'s mooring lines. The ship drifted toward *Titanic*. A collision seemed imminent. Tugs managed to keep the two ships apart by just a few feet.

The stokers had one of the hardest jobs on board the *Titanic*.

They continually shoveled heavy loads of coal into the furnaces that fed the boilers. The boilers generated the steam that was responsible for propelling the ship.

Titanic crossed the English Channel to Cherbourg, France. No dock could accommodate her. She had to lie offshore. A few passengers got off the ship. More than 200 boarded. Later that evening she sailed for Queenstown, Ireland. She arrived the next morning. Again her huge size forced her to lie offshore. About 120 passengers boarded the vessel. Seven departed. At 1:00 P.M. on Thursday, April 11, *Titanic* got under way. She was scheduled to arrive in New York early the following Wednesday.

That day and the next two passed uneventfully. The seas were unusually calm. Each day the ship covered more miles than it had the previous day. The passengers enjoyed the shipboard amenities. There was nothing to disturb them. Not even a lifeboat drill.

Perhaps the most famous *Titanic* survivor was Margaret "Maggie" Brown. She was later featured in a musical and movie entitled *The Unsinkable Molly Brown*. According to the film, she had been a singer and dancer in a Western saloon when she married James J. Brown, a very rich man. This portrayal isn't very accurate. Even the title is wrong. She was never known as Molly.

Margaret Tobin was born in Hannibal, Missouri, in 1867. She grew up in poverty, but her family was close-knit. She attended school until she was thirteen. Then she went to work for a tobacco company.

A few years later, she moved to Leadville, Colorado, a rough mining town. Margaret wanted to marry a rich man so that she could help her family. Soon she met James J. Brown. He didn't have much money, but she married him anyway. They had two children.

A scene from the movie *The Unsinkable Molly Brown*

Brown invented a way of strengthening mine shafts. His invention helped uncover a great deal of gold. The Browns became very rich. They moved to Denver and lived in a large mansion. Margaret became socially prominent.

As a wealthy woman, Margaret was expected to be active in charity. She went beyond all expectations. She had a reputation for being very generous.

Unfortunately, there were strains in the marriage. Some came about because Margaret was very forceful. She became active politically, which was unusual for a woman in that time. The couple separated in 1909. Soon afterward, Margaret went to Europe. She returned on *Titanic*. As people began abandoning ship, she helped load lifeboats. A crewman picked her up and threw her into another lifeboat. She helped row it away from danger.

She comforted the survivors as the ship that rescued them headed for New York. There she provided financial help for many of them.

After the sinking, her life became even more active. She ran for the U.S. Senate at a time when women didn't have the right to vote. She campaigned for women's rights. She volunteered to help in Europe during World War I. She traveled. She even became an actress.

Margaret Brown lived her last years in a hotel room in New York City. She died in 1932.

Crewmen of the rescue ship *Carpathia* he
operator Harold Bride off the ship in

Bride stayed with Titanic as long as he could, sending out distress messages. He suffered severe frostbite to his feet because of the cold water.

CHAPTER 3

The Fateful Day

On Sunday morning, April 14, the shipboard routine began as usual. There was a church service. The passengers enjoyed a sumptuous lunch. Everything seemed normal.

Things weren't quite as normal in the ship's radio room. Radio operators Jack Phillips and Harold Bride began receiving ice warnings from other ships. The first one came in at 9:00 A.M. from the Cunard liner *Caronia*. She reported an ice field studded with icebergs. The field stretched along two degrees of longitude—about sixty miles. It was directly in *Titanic*'s path.

Ships had begun carrying radios, or wireless telegraphs, about a decade earlier. At that time, voice communication wasn't possible. The operators tapped out messages in Morse code. Each letter was represented by a combination of dots (short taps on the transmitter key) and dashes (longer taps). For example, *A* is represented as a dot and a dash. *B* is a dash and three dots. *C* is a dash, a dot, and another dash and dot. Transmitting in Morse code was relatively slow. Even the best operators rarely sent more than twenty words a minute.

Wireless was still largely regarded as a novelty. Most people considered its primary use as sending messages from passengers to their friends on shore. The system often was unreliable. Reception depended on atmospheric conditions. There were no guarantees of being able to reach shore stations. The equipment itself often broke down. There was no standard procedure for notifying the ships' officers of incoming messages.

Few—if any—of the passengers were aware of the increasingly ominous ice reports that filtered into *Titanic*'s radio room. Just before noon, the Dutch ship *Noordam* reported high concentrations of ice at about the same location as the *Caronia*. A third message came in two hours later from the *Baltic*. The ship reported ice about 250 miles directly ahead of *Titanic*. Smith looked at the message. He wasn't surprised. He knew that he would probably encounter ice. He didn't seem worried.

Ismay was on the bridge at the time. Smith gave him the message. Ismay put it in his pocket. Later he showed it to two first-class passengers. Apparently he was trying to impress them with the ship's power and safety.

Moments later, the German liner *Amerika* reported a large iceberg. The message never left *Titanic*'s radio room.

The afternoon went by peacefully. Shortly before six o'clock, Smith slightly altered course to the south and west. He may have believed that this maneuver would carry the ship south of the ice that had been reported.

Titanic's evening routine began. The passengers ate dinner, played cards, read, talked with their friends. Some strolled along the decks.

At 7:30, Smith attended a dinner in his honor. A few minutes later, the *Californian* sent a warning. The ship was proceeding in the same direction as *Titanic* but was a little ahead and slightly to the north. She radioed a report of three good-sized icebergs three miles to the south. Captain Smith never got this message.

An hour later, Second Officer Herbert Lightoller told some crew members to keep an eye on the ship's fresh water supply. In a little over an hour, the temperature had gone from the mid-40s to just above freezing. He wanted to make sure that the fresh water didn't freeze.

Soon afterward, Smith excused himself. He went to the bridge. He and Lightoller talked for several minutes. Smith told Lightoller he was going to bed. He emphasized that Lightoller should call him immediately if there was any sign of danger.

He didn't tell Lightoller to slow down. It was customary for ships in areas of ice to sail as close to their top speed as they could. Most captains believed that their lookouts could see ice in plenty of time to avoid it. Smith shared this belief. There was also a practical reason. Ships respond more quickly to their helm when they are going faster.

Smith knew he would generate bad publicity if he slowed down or even stopped. It would be a public admission that the ship's officers were afraid of ice. He certainly didn't want to be compared with someone like James Clayton Barr, the captain of the *Caronia*. Most officers on the North Atlantic route thought he was too cautious. They said he slowed down any-time there was haze. They gave him the nickname Foggy.[1] It wasn't meant as a compliment.

There was another reason for Captain Smith's apparent lack of cau-tion. He hadn't been shown or even told of all the incoming ice messages. He apparently assumed that his ship was south of the ice that had been reported. If so, it was a fatal assumption. He wasn't alone. None of the other officers had seen all the messages, either.

Smith might have ordered Lightoller to station additional lookouts. He didn't. There were already two in the crow's nest high up on the fore-mast. They were the only ones keeping watch for danger ahead. None of the seven men on the bridge had the specific responsibility to act as a lookout. Nor was anyone ordered forward to the bow. Bow lookouts would have had a different perspective than the men in the crow's nest. It might have been easier for them to see danger silhouetted against the black sky.

No one knows if Lightoller commented about the sudden drop in temperature. Noted Antarctic explorer Ernest Shackleton was a national hero for his gallant efforts to reach the South Pole. His experiences had given him firsthand knowledge of icebergs. "If there was no wind and the temperature fell abnormally for the time of the year, I would consider that I was approaching an area which might have ice in it,"[2] he said later.

A few minutes after Captain Smith left, another message crackled into Phillips's earphones. It was from the steamer *Mesaba*. The ship re-ported large icebergs and field ice. The position was directly in front of *Titanic*. Phillips never gave the report to the officers on the bridge. One reason may have been that it didn't start with *MSG*. That stood for "Masters' Service Gram." MSG messages required the captain's signature.

At about 11:00, the *Californian* sent a message. She had stopped for the night. Proceeding further would have been too risky, Captain Stanley

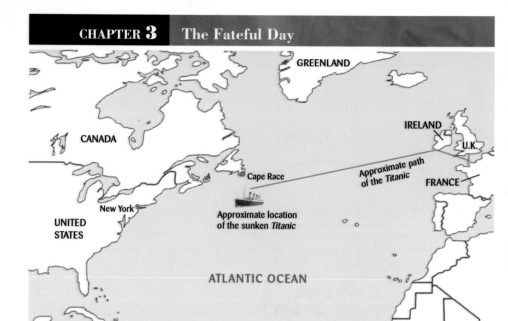

After stopping in France and Ireland, *Titanic* steamed across the Atlantic. Only about one-third of the passengers and crew members arrived at New York, the ship's intended destination. Cape Race is the shore station that heard the *Titanic's* anguished pleas for assistance.

Lord decided. The ship's radio operator, Cyril Evans, knew *Titanic* was nearby. Evans wanted to alert *Titanic* about how close she was to the ice field. But he made a mistake. He didn't give his message the MSG prefix either. He began, "Say, old man, we are stopped and surrounded by ice."[3]

 Californian was so close—less than twenty miles away—that the transmission was very loud in Phillips's ear. It was almost painful in its intensity. Phillips was furious. Passengers had bombarded him all day with messages to send to their friends ashore, and he got paid for every message he sent. He had just managed to contact a shore station at Cape Race. It is located in Newfoundland, Canada. At last he could begin dispatching the mound of messages in front of him.

 He immediately began pounding the telegraph key. "Shut up, shut up. I am busy," he replied. "I am working Cape Race."[4]

 In just over an hour, Phillips would again be "working Cape Race. " By then, passenger messages to their friends would be the furthest thing from his mind.

As soon as people began venturing into the world's oceans, one problem became apparent. When a ship disappeared over the horizon, there was no way of keeping track of it. Most ships made it safely to their destinations. Some didn't. Many vanished without leaving a trace.

In 1844, Samuel F. B. Morse successfully demonstrated his telegraph. He sent a message from Washington, D.C., to Baltimore, Maryland. Telegraph wires soon stretched across vast distances. However, Morse's invention was useless for ships. They couldn't drag hundreds of miles of telegraph wires behind them.

Guglielmo Marconi

While many researchers made vital contributions, the development of a practical system of what became known as wireless telegraphy owed the most to Italian inventor Guglielmo Marconi. Born in 1874, Marconi became interested in electricity at a young age. When he was twenty, he had the idea that would make him famous: using electromagnetic waves to send messages. Electromagnetic waves are a combination of electricity and magnetism. They travel at the speed of light. Radio waves, microwaves, and X-rays are several types of electromagnetic waves. These waves don't need wires.

At first Marconi sent his electromagnetic signals across an attic room. Then he moved outdoors. Soon he was transmitting and receiving at distances of more than a mile. His greatest work came when he moved to England. In 1901, he sent a signal across the Atlantic Ocean.

He formed a company to take advantage of the commercial possibilities of his invention. He became so famous that *marconi* became a synonym for *wireless telegraphy*. People often referred to telegrams as marconigrams.

In 1909, he received the world's highest honor for his work. It was the Nobel Prize for Physics. The timing was especially significant. Earlier that year, two passenger ships—the *Republic* and the *Florida*—collided near New York. The *Republic*'s radio operator sent out a distress signal. Nearby ships quickly converged on the scene. They rescued nearly everyone. It was the first time that radio saved lives at sea. It would be far from the last.

Marconi and his family almost sailed on *Titanic*. They had accepted an invitation to join the maiden voyage. At the last minute, Marconi realized he had to get to New York before the ship's scheduled arrival. He took another ship instead. His wife had to cancel because her son was ill. She watched as *Titanic* departed without her.

The lifeboats are lowered after the with an iceberg.

The first lifeboats to leave the ship were far short of capacity. It wasn't immediately obvious to the passengers that they were in danger.

"Iceberg Right Ahead"

Lookouts Fred Fleet and Reginald Lee had come on duty at ten o'clock. They were stationed in the crow's nest on the foremast, high above the deck. It was especially difficult duty. The air temperature hovered just above freezing. The ship's forward motion created a biting wind that blew directly into their faces. It probably made their eyes water. As the night wore on, they began looking forward to being relieved at midnight. They would enjoy a hot drink. Then they would go to sleep in a warm cabin.

Both men were experienced lookouts. That was their primary duty on board the ship. They received extra pay for their skill.

A little after 11:30, Fleet and Lee spotted what appeared to be a dim white haze ahead of the ship. The haze extended several miles north and south of the ship's westerly course. They couldn't check it out further. They didn't have any binoculars. Someone had misplaced them before the ship left Southampton.

At 11:40, Fleet suddenly saw something dead ahead. At first he thought it was small, about the size of two tables placed end to end. Then he realized it was considerably larger. Author Walter Lord recorded the story:

> Quickly Fleet banged the crow's-nest bell three times, the warning of danger ahead. At the same time he lifted the phone and rang the bridge.
>
> "What did you see?" asked a calm voice at the other end.
>
> "Iceberg right ahead," replied Fleet.
>
> "Thank you," acknowledged the voice with curiously detached courtesy. Nothing more was said.[1]

First officer William Murdoch had come on duty at ten o'clock. He acted instinctively. He ordered a hard turn to port. A turning ship doesn't act the same way as a turning car. Turning the bow away from the berg would slide the stern toward it. Murdoch knew he would have to quickly turn the ship in the opposite direction as soon as the bow cleared the obstruction. That would swing the stern away.

Murdoch's orders may have condemned more than 1,500 people—including himself—to death.

While comparatively rare, collisions with icebergs weren't unknown. Many ships disappeared without a trace in the days before wireless telegraphy. Anyone who fell into the icy waters of the North Atlantic would be dead within a few minutes. The sea would quickly swallow up the remains.

Some ships survived their encounters. If they struck the berg head-on, the impact would crumple the bow, but only the far forward compartments would fill with seawater. If the bulkheads managed to hold, the ship would remain afloat indefinitely. This very thing had occurred thirty-three years earlier. The liner *Arizona* plowed into an iceberg. The bow was crumpled. The ship survived. She managed to limp to safety.

Murdoch didn't have any time to debate the issue. As a very experienced seaman, his deeply ingrained instinct was to avoid a head-on collision. He also knew that hundreds of third-class passengers and crewmen were asleep in the front part of the ship. Hitting the berg would kill many and maim even more.

Murdoch hoped his maneuver would twist the bow around the iceberg. Then he would spin the wheel in the opposite direction. The bow would pass beyond the iceberg as the stern also cleared the danger.

There simply wasn't enough time. By the time Fleet saw the berg and got word to the bridge, there was less than a minute until impact. *Titanic* did avoid a head-on collision. Instead, the berg scraped across much of the forward one-third of the ship. Five compartments began to fill with water.

Most of the passengers were asleep. They didn't feel the collision. The ones who were awake weren't knocked off their feet. One reported a gentle thump. Another compared the sensation to rolling over marbles. A few even thought that the ship had dropped its anchor for some reason. Or perhaps a propeller blade had fallen off. Hardly anyone was concerned.

Some even thought it was a treat. Chunks of the berg fell onto the foredeck. The few passengers who were there reportedly played soccer with the smaller fragments. Other passengers were enjoying a final cocktail in the ship's lounge. They jokingly asked their friends to go forward and grab some ice to freshen their drinks.

On the bridge, Captain Smith wasn't playing any games. He quickly summoned Thomas Andrews. Andrews was a Harland and Wolff official. He hadn't been scheduled to make the voyage. Pirrie became ill so Andrews sailed in his place. He made an inspection of the foremost compartments. He returned with horrifying news. *Titanic* had less than two hours to live.

Under some circumstances, *Titanic* could survive with as many as four compartments flooded. Not five. That was because the "watertight compartments" weren't really watertight at all. As undersea explorer Robert Ballard explains, "The bulkheads stood barely 15 feet above the waterline. As the ocean filled the fifth compartment, the weight dragged the bow low enough for water to slop over the top of the bulkhead and into the sixth. When the sixth filled, it flooded the seventh, and so on in a chain reaction, like filling an ice cube tray from one end with the spillover flowing toward the other."[2]

Smith didn't waste any time. He ordered Phillips and Bride to transmit distress signals. The first one went out shortly after midnight.

That began a desperate race against time. A number of ships and shore stations such as Cape Race received the signal. One ship was *Olympic*. She was on her way back to England, but she was 560 miles away. Even at top speed, she would need nearly a full day to reach her sister. Much closer was the *Carpathia*, a small Cunard liner en route to the Mediterranean. She was just 58 miles away. Captain Arthur Rostron turned his ship around. He ordered top speed. He even turned off the heat in the passenger cabins to provide more steam to turn the propellers. Even so, he knew it would take more than three hours to arrive.

He was aware of the danger into which he was putting his ship and his passengers. As a safety measure, he ordered two men to the bow to serve as additional lookouts. He also ordered two more men onto the bridge to watch for ice.

The *Californian* was lying much closer, but she didn't hear the desperate signal. After being brushed off by Phillips, Evans had turned off his set at 11:35. Then he went to sleep. He was the ship's only radio operator.

At about 12:45, Smith ordered the firing of distress rockets. *Californian*'s officers saw them. In all likelihood, they also saw the *Titanic*, but they probably weren't sure what they were seeing. The giant ship's desperate maneuvers presented several different "looks." If Captain Lord had awakened Evans, the radioman would immediately have grasped the situation. Lord didn't want to disturb Evans. He knew the man was exhausted. *Californian* stayed where she was.

Back on the *Titanic*, people were slowly starting to get into the lifeboats. Captain Smith had chosen not to give an Abandon Ship order. He wanted to avoid panic and hundreds of people stampeding to the boats. Instead, he ordered the lifeboats to be uncovered. The officers in charge of loading the lifeboats tried to uphold the old tradition of the sea: Women and children first. That may have been a mistake. Some women refused to leave without their husbands. Others were afraid of being in boats without any men to row. Somewhat reluctantly, the officers allowed a few male passengers and crew members lucky enough to be in the vicinity into the boats.

The process was further slowed because very few members of the crew knew where they were supposed to be. After all, there hadn't been any lifeboat drills.

The first boat wasn't launched until 12:45 A.M. Only 27 people were aboard. It had room for at least 40 more. Another contained just 12. Even an hour after the collision, people were reluctant to leave the seeming safety of the ship. Eventually more and more began to grasp that the ship was doomed. Nearly all of the later boats were filled.

Many, if not most, of the men who stayed behind behaved honorably. Benjamin Guggenheim went below to put on formal wear in order to die like a gentleman. Archibald Butts, a friend of President William Howard Taft, joined three other men for a card game. Astor put his eighteen-year-old bride into one of the last remaining boats. There was room for at least a

Guggenheim and his valet sat in deck chairs as the ship went down. His daughter, Peggy, would use the fortune he left her to become a world-famous art collector.

Benjamin Guggenheim, a banking and mining millionaire, was aboard the _Titanic_.

dozen more people. Astor asked the officer in charge if he could join his wife. The officer shook his head. Astor politely stepped back. No one else stepped forward to enter the boat. It pulled away from the ship with the empty spots.

The eight members of the ship's band became legendary for providing music up until the ship's final moments. None of them survived. Neither did Phillips. He remained at his post sending out distress messages until the end. Nor did Captain Smith. There were several versions of the manner in which he died. No one knows for sure.

Some men survived by being in the right place at the right time. Lawrence Beesley, a thirty-four-year-old schoolteacher, was leaning over the railing. A lifeboat immediately below him was almost ready to be launched. The officer in charge called for any more ladies. None responded. He looked up and saw Beesley.

"Are there any ladies on your deck?" he said.

An artist's impression of *Titanic*'s final moments.

The smoke from the funnels shows that stokers were still working. Their work allowed the ship's lights to remain on until the ship finally sank.

"No," [Beesley] replied.

"Then you had better jump."[3]

Ismay may have found himself in a similar situation. When he was picked up a few hours later, he explained that he had helped to load some of the lifeboats. As one of the final ones was being lowered, he looked around. He didn't see any passengers, so he stepped aboard. Some witnesses say that he pushed and shoved his way past a number of other men.

The last two boats were mounted on top of the bridge. They were washed away as the water level reached that high. Several dozen men clung desperately to them. Just over 700 people had managed to escape the sinking vessel. Fifteen hundred more remained aboard.

At about 2:20 A.M., Titanic slipped beneath the waves. No one would see her again for more than seven decades.

Plans to salvage *Titanic* began to surface almost immediately after her sinking. There were rumors of large amounts of money that had gone down with the ship. Nothing came of these plans. Existing technology was hopelessly inadequate for the task. The wreckage lay under two and a half miles of water.

There was another problem. Nobody knew exactly where the wreckage lay. The position sent out in the distress signal was wrong. The officer who had calculated it was under a lot of pressure. He made several errors.

Robert Ballard

Decades later, a number of people wanted to locate the wreckage. One was an American scientist named Robert Ballard. His first effort in 1977 ended with a major equipment failure.

A wealthy oilman named Jack Grimm tried to find *Titanic* three times during the early 1980s. He wasn't successful either.

Ballard didn't give up. He spent several years seeking financial support. He tried again in 1985. By then the U.S. Navy had successfully developed deep-diving unmanned undersea research vehicles. These vehicles sent back television pictures. The navy allowed Ballard to use their equipment.

Ballard had a large area to search. The research ship they were using couldn't go very fast. It was dull work. For hours on end, the pictures sent back from the bottom were virtually unchanged. Only an occasional fish or boulder came into view.

In the early morning hours of September 1, the half-asleep operators suddenly got very excited. The submersibles were sending back pictures of manmade objects on the ocean floor. Then they saw a ship's boiler. They had found *Titanic*! Ballard felt that he had found something more than just wreckage.

"Here at the bottom of the ocean lay not only the graveyard of a great ship, but the only fitting monument to the more than 1500 people who had perished when she went down," he wrote. "And we were the very first people in 73 years to come to this precise spot to pay our respects."[4]

The following year Ballard went down to the site in a small manned submarine. Since then, other people have also visited the ship. Seeing the wreckage is always a very emotional experience.

The photo of *Titanic*'s sunken bow is one of the most famous shots taken during Robert Ballard's expedition.

Ballard fears that corrosion will eventually cause the wreckage to collapse.

How Could Such a Horrible Event Happen?

Titanic was gone. The people in the lifeboats had to deal with a fresh horror. Probably only a few hundred people actually went down with the ship. More than a thousand were in the water in their lifejackets. They were screaming in agony as the bitterly cold water began choking off their lives. They pleaded for help.

Many people in the rowboats wanted to go back and pick them up. The crewmen in charge of the boats refused. If they went back, they explained, dozens of desperate people would try to climb aboard. They would swamp the fragile boats. Everyone would die. There was nothing to be done—except listen. Finally the last plaintive cries faded out. Miraculously, a few in the water survived. One was Archibald Gracie. The suction of the sinking ship pulled him under the water. An air bubble popped him to the surface. He scrambled to safety on one of the boats. The huddled survivors in Gracie's boat joined those in the other nineteen as they waited for rescue.

They didn't have to wait long. Around 4:00 A.M., the *Carpathia* appeared in the morning twilight. It was too dangerous for her to maneuver through the ice-choked ocean. One by one, the lifeboats rowed to the ship. By 8:00 A.M., all the survivors were on board.

About 200 of them were first-class passengers. They represented 60 percent of the first-class passengers who had boarded the ship. From second-class, 120 (or 42 percent) survived. Just 175 third-class passengers were rescued—a survival rate of 25 percent. The crew members' survival rate was about the same as third class. Two hundred fourteen of them lived.

Many people believe that these different survival rates show a bias in favor of wealthier passengers. That isn't necessarily true. For one thing, first-class passengers occupied the staterooms that were closest to the lifeboats. For another, they were more likely to be awake that late in the evening. Third-class passengers were encouraged to be in their rooms by 10:00 P.M., so many weren't even aware that there was trouble. Most of their rooms were deep in the rear of the ship. There were also gates between them and the rest of the ship. It was more difficult for them to get to the lifeboats.

By the time *Carpathia* had finished taking the survivors, other ships had arrived on the scene. There was little for them to do. Some picked up bodies from the water. This gruesome chore would continue for over two months. More than 300 corpses were recovered. The rest vanished.

The disaster became front-page news all over the world. People wanted answers, and they wanted them immediately. Even before the *Carpathia* arrived in New York, the U.S. Senate had decided to conduct an investigation. So the did the British Board of Trade.

Each investigation began with a bias. The Americans wanted to throw the blame on the British. The British returned the favor.

The American investigation got under way on April 19. Michigan Senator William Alden Smith was the driving force. He wanted to get started immediately. The survivors had landed the night before, and he didn't want anyone to leave before he or she could be questioned. The interviews began in the Waldorf-Astoria hotel. Three days later the scene shifted to Washington, D.C. The chief value of the investigation would be the number of people Smith and the other committee members could question.

Smith's investigation left more questions remaining than it answered. For one thing, Smith had little practical knowledge of maritime matters. As a result, his primary focus was on the lack of lifeboats. He recorded relatively few details about the actual sinking.

Many people hoped that the British investigation would provide some of these details. They would be disappointed. The British Board of Trade was the very group that had established the lifeboat formula which enabled *Titanic*'s defenders to claim that they had actually surpassed the legal requirements. It had also certified the ship after her abbreviated sea trials. If

White Star Line was found at fault, it would damage the reputation of other British shipping lines. This finding would also open the line to liability for millions of dollars in lawsuits.

As a result, "this investigation was not an attempt to get to the bottom of the story, but to sanitize it and remove its sting," *Titanic* historian Don Lynch points out. "Apart from protecting itself, the [Board of Trade] had no interest in seeing the White Star Line found negligent."[1]

Many years later, Second Officer Lightoller expressed a similar feeling. "Sharp questions needed careful answers if one was to avoid . . . a pinning down of blame to someone's luckless shoulders," he wrote. "A washing of dirty linen would help no one. The Board of Trade had passed that ship as in all respects fit for sea, in every sense of the word, with sufficient margin of safety for everyone on board. Now, the Board of Trade was holding an inquiry into the loss of that ship—hence the whitewash."[2]

Not surprisingly, the Board of Trade let Ismay off the hook. "Had he [Ismay] not jumped in he would simply have added one more life, namely his own, to the number of those lost,"[3] the report stated.

While Ismay wasn't guilty of any actual crimes, he was guilty in the court of public opinion. Many people condemned him for not going down with the ship. American newspapers were especially harsh with him. Some identified him as "J. Brute Ismay."[4] Others wrote, "We respectfully suggest that the emblem of the White Star be changed to that of a yellow liver."[5]

Ismay was forced to resign as chairman of White Star Line.

Some people believe that the line was at fault for claiming that *Titanic* was unsinkable. White Star never made such a claim. Nor did Harland and Wolff. Rather, the claim came from newspapers and magazines. In turn, they were reflecting what their readers *wanted* to believe. For the company to have contradicted the claim—to have said something like, "No, the papers are wrong, any ship can sink"—would have been business suicide.

And like nearly everyone living in that era, they probably went along with the idea. As the U.S. investigation noted, "Science in shipbuilding was supposed to have attained perfection and to have spoken her last word."[6]

Captain Smith shared the same opinion. "I cannot conceive of any disaster happening to this vessel," he said of one of his earlier commands.

Article from *The Rocky Mountain News* about the sinking of the *Titanic*.

This is typical of the sensational media coverage of the tragedy. It made front-page news around the world.

"Modern shipbuilding has gone beyond all that."[7] Commanding *Titanic* would have increased this sense of invulnerability.

One controversy erupted during the investigations. Many passengers and some crew members insisted that the ship broke apart just before it sank. The surviving officers apparently got together before they had to testify. They all agreed to testify that the ship had remained intact. It was bad enough that "unsinkable" *Titanic* had sunk. If people suspected the ship was so weak that it had broken apart, many would be unwilling to travel on *Olympic* and the still incomplete *Britannic*.

Robert Ballard resolved the controversy in 1985. He found the two sections far apart on the bottom. It was obvious that the ship had broken before sinking.

The two investigations agreed on at least two points. One was that Captain Rostron of *Carpathia* was a hero. He became a knight. He could refer to himself as Sir Arthur Rostron. When Cunard and White Star merged in 1934, he was named the company's honorary commodore.

The other was their scapegoat. They knew public opinion demanded a villain as well as a hero. Captain Lord of the *Californian* was an ideal target. Senator Smith wrote that Lord "failed to respond to [*Titanic's* signals] in accordance with the dictates of humanity, international usage, and the requirements of law. . . . In our opinion such conduct, whether arising from indifference or gross carelessness, is most reprehensible."[8]

The British added, "When she first saw the rockets the *Californian* could have pushed through the ice to the open water without any serious risk and so have come to the assistance of the *Titanic*. Had she done so she might have saved many if not all of the lives that were lost."[9]

From Lord's point of view, heading toward the rockets would have posed a very serious safety risk. He knew he was nearly surrounded by large icebergs. His ship was only half as long as *Titanic*. It weighed slightly over 6,000 tons. He had no illusions that it was "unsinkable."

Not only that, he and his officers weren't sure they were seeing a ship in distress. They tried to make contact using a high-powered light that sent signals in Morse code. It was useless. The ships were too far away.

Ballard's discovery of *Titanic* provided evidence that Lord was not guilty of any wrongdoing. Since *Californian* had been stopped for so long, her navigator was able to determine her exact position. On the other hand, *Titanic's* actual position was 13 miles farther southeast—and 13 miles farther away from *Californian*—than the one her frantic radio operators were transmitting. Even if Lord had responded immediately, *Titanic* would have foundered by the time he arrived.

This condemnation of Lord contrasts with the treatment of *Titanic's* surviving officers. Especially in England, their actions were regarded heroically. Lord worked for Leyland Lines and was forced to resign.

The shipping industry in general had a much different point of view. Lord wasn't unemployed very long. A few months after his resignation, another company hired him to command one of their ships. He had a long career with them. *Titanic's* officers never achieved civilian command. Nor did they serve on any other prestigious ships.

The two investigations resulted in a number of recommendations. The most obvious was that ships must carry enough lifeboats for everyone.

Pictures of *Olympic* taken a few years later show three layers of lifeboats on each side. The U.S. Coast Guard International Ice Patrol was founded in 1913. Radio operators were ordered to give top priority to any messages that concerned their ship's operation and safety. To speed delivery of these vital communications, ships were urged to install pneumatic tubes that ran directly from the radio room to the bridge. That way the ship's officers would immediately receive incoming messages. Ships were also required to have a radio operator on duty twenty-four hours a day.

Many people point fingers at Captain Smith in particular and White Star Line in general. Passenger Beesley noted: "It would seem as if [Captain Smith] deliberately ran his ship . . . through a region infested with icebergs, and did a thing which no one has ever done before; that he outraged all precedent by not slowing down. But it is plain that he did not."[10]

He continued, "So that it is the custom that is at fault, not one particular captain. Custom is established largely by demand. . . . The public has demanded, more and more every year, greater speed as well as greater comfort, and by ceasing to patronize the low-speed boats has gradually forced the pace to what it is at present."[11]

The respected magazine *Harper's Weekly* made the same point. "We are all to blame for the wreck of the *Titanic*," its editors wrote. "Not Captain Smith alone—gallant man—not her owners only, but the dominating spirit of our time, to which each of us contributes his quota of impatience."[12]

Titanic was unfortunate. Hundreds of factors—the vast majority of them seemingly trivial—combined to put her in the wrong place at the wrong time. Some didn't even involve the ship itself. For example, the two times that *Olympic* was damaged sent her back to Belfast. Resources and workers were shifted from work on *Titanic* to repair *Olympic*. That prevented *Titanic* from sailing on the original date of her maiden voyage in mid-March. If she had, the iceberg danger would still have existed, but the odds are that her voyage would have been uneventful.

She became the symbol of the futility of man's belief in the supremacy of his own achievements. That was precisely why Robertson chose *Futility* as the title of his book. In an era that worshiped progress and technology, he was one of the few people who thought otherwise.

The steering motor from the bridge of the *Titanic* slowly corrodes undersea.

The helmsman furiously spun the ship's wheel, activating the steering motor, in an effort to avoid the iceberg. There simply wasn't enough time to avoid it.

The rest of the twentieth century and the early part of the twenty-first witnessed unparalleled technological accomplishments. These accomplishments have led many people to have the same sort of faith in the ability of human beings to control and dominate their environment as J. Bruce Ismay, Lord William Pirrie, and Captain Edward Smith did.

In 2005, most residents of New Orleans believed that technology had rendered them safe from the ravages of nature. Levees held back the Mississippi River. Millions of acres of protective swampland and timberland that acted as natural buffers were eliminated due to development.

Then Hurricane Katrina swept through the area. The levees crumbled. Flooding became far worse because so much of the surrounding countryside had been built up. As a result, Hurricane Katrina became the worst natural disaster in American history.

The lessons learned from the sinking of *Titanic* are just as valuable today as they were in 1912.

The sequence of events in the previous chapters has long been accepted as the explanation for *Titanic*'s loss. In 2001, David G. Brown published *The Last Log of the Titanic*. Unlike most previous authors, Brown is an experienced seaman. His book differs from the standard account in many particulars.

One of the most important is that *Titanic* didn't run *into* an iceberg. She ran *over* an iceberg. A tongue of hard ice jutted out from the submerged part of the berg. *Titanic* rumbled over the tongue.

Brown's most controversial idea is that the damage was *not* fatal. He agrees that water flooded several forward compartments, but pumps would have been able to keep up with the flow. What doomed the ship came a few minutes after the collision.

Smith ordered the vessel to resume steaming. The forward motion forced more water into the ship. Now the pumps couldn't keep up. Water levels climbed. The ship was doomed when water spilled over from the fifth damaged compartment into the one behind it.

Noted *Titanic* historian Walter Lord writes that at least three crewmen say that the ship steamed forward after the collision. "Many passengers, too, recall the ship starting ahead again, mostly because it seemed so comforting."[14]

Indeed they were. Beesley commented, "The ship had now resumed her course, moving very slowly through the water with a little white line of foam on each side. I think we were all glad to see this; it seemed better than standing still."[15]

Brown's viewpoint gains further strength from the two investigations.

Five days after the accident, Ismay told the U.S. Senate about a conversation with chief engineer Joseph Bell. "I asked if [Bell] thought the ship was seriously damaged, and he said he thought she was. But [he] was satisfied the pumps would keep her afloat."[16]

The final report from the British commission states, "Even if the four forward compartments had been flooded the water would not have got into any of the compartments abaft of [behind] them . . . the ship, even with these four compartments flooded, would have remained afloat."[17]

Brown doesn't claim that the ship wouldn't have eventually sunk. He does claim that it would have remained afloat at least a few hours longer. For more than 1,500 people, that could have made the difference between life and death.

It's unlikely that we'll have a final answer. Much of the wreckage is buried under many feet of mud.

Chronology

1907   White Star Line chairman J. Bruce Ismay and Lord William Pirrie of Harland and Wolff Shipyard decide to build three large ocean liners, emphasizing luxury rather than speed

1909   *Titanic*'s first keel plate is laid down in Harland and Wolff Shipyard

1911   *Titanic* is launched

1912

January	*Titanic*'s interior is completed
February	*Titanic*'s three propellers are installed
April 2	*Titanic* conducts sea trials
April 10	*Titanic* leaves Southampton, England; stops briefly at Cherbourg, France, to take on passengers and departs later that night for Queenstown, Ireland
April 11	*Titanic* takes on more passengers at Queenstown; leaves at 1:30 P.M. on her maiden voyage across the Atlantic

April 14

9:00 A.M.	*Titanic* receives first iceberg warning
11:00 P.M.	*Titanic* receives final iceberg warning
11:40 P.M.	*Titanic* strikes iceberg

April 15

12:15 A.M.	Radio operators begin sending distress signal
12:45 A.M.	*Titanic* launches distress rockets; first lifeboat leaves ship
2:20 A.M.	*Titanic* sinks
4:10 A.M.	*Carpathia* picks up first lifeboat
8:00 A.M.	*Carpathia* completes rescue of survivors

April 18	Survivors arrive in New York City
April 19	U.S. Senate committee begins hearings about the loss of *Titanic*
May 2	British Board of Trade begins investigation of *Titanic* sinking

1913   J. Bruce Ismay is forced to resign as chairman of White Star Line

1932   Margaret Brown dies at the age of 65

1985   Ocean explorer Robert Ballard discovers the wreck of *Titanic*

1997   Director James Cameron's award-winning film *Titanic* is released

2001   Two people are married in a submersible near *Titanic* wreck site

2005   Groundbreaking begins on the Titanic Quarter, a $20 billion commercial and residential project in Belfast, Northern Ireland; it includes a *Titanic* museum, scheduled to open in 2011

Timeline in History

1807   Robert Fulton's steamboat *Clermont* begins regular passenger service on New York's Hudson River.

1819   SS *Savannah* becomes the first steamship to make a transatlantic crossing, though the vessel uses her sails for much of the trip.

1838   British vessels *Great Western* and *Sirius* become first two ships to cross the Atlantic using only steam power.

1839   Sir Samuel Cunard signs contract to deliver transatlantic mail using steamships.

1840   Cunard Line is first to offer regularly scheduled transatlantic passenger service.

1845   The White Star Line is founded in Liverpool, England.

1848   SS *California* inaugurates steamship travel between the east and west coasts of the United States; the voyage around Cape Horn lasts nearly five months.

1862   USS *Monitor* and CSS *Virginia* clash during the Civil War in history's first battle between two armored steamships.

1863   White Star Line acquires its first steamship, the *Royal Standard*.

1864   *Royal Standard* strikes an iceberg and suffers major damage but is able to arrive in port.

1868   Thomas Ismay and Edward Harland buy the struggling White Star Line.

1871   White Star Line's "greatest triumph," the SS *Oceanic*, enters service.

1881   *Servia* becomes the first all-steel commercial vessel.

1901   Cunard liner *Lucania* becomes the first commercial vessel to carry wireless telegraph.

1902   U.S. financier J. Pierpont Morgan purchases the White Star Line; its ships continue to fly the British flag and to be manned by British crews.

1911   *Titanic*'s sister ship *Olympic* makes maiden voyage to New York.

1913   The International Ice Patrol is organized; its purpose is to monitor North Atlantic ice conditions.

1914   *Titanic*'s other sister ship, *Britannic*, is launched.

1916   *Britannic* sinks after striking a mine, but most of the people aboard survive.

1934   White Star Line and Cunard Line merge.

1935   *Olympic* is removed from active service and sold for scrap.

1940   British liner *Lancastria* sinks after being attacked by German bombers while evacuating troops from France; several thousand people perish.

1958   American ship *Savannah* becomes the first nuclear-powered commercial vessel; its operating costs are too high and the ship soon goes out of service.

1969   Cunard liner *Queen Elizabeth II* enters service; the vessel becomes the first vessel to sail 5 million nautical miles.

1992   *Queen Elizabeth II* strikes a rock near Massachusetts; no one is injured or killed; passengers describe a very similar sensation on impact as *Titanic* survivors.

2003   Harland and Wolff Company stops building ships.

2004   Cunard liner *Queen Mary II* begins transatlantic service; the new ship is the largest and most expensive ocean liner ever built.

2006   Royal Caribbean liner *Freedom of the Seas* is launched; at 158,000 tons, it surpasses the *Queen Mary II* as the largest ocean liner. Western Union announces it will discontinue its telegraphy services.

Chapter Notes

Chapter 1 Built to Be Unsinkable

1. Tom McCluskie, Michael Sharpe, and Leo Marriott, Titanic *and Her Sisters* Olympic *and* Britannic (San Diego, CA: Thunder Bay Press, 1998), p. 56.

2. Robert D. Ballard with Michael S. Sweeney, *Return to* Titanic: *A New Look at the World's Most Famous Lost Ship* (Washington, D.C.: National Geographic, 2004), p. 20.

3. Wyn Craig Wade, *The* Titanic: *End of a Dream* (New York: Penguin Books, 1986), p. 288.

4. Proverbs 16:18, King James Version.

Chapter 2 The Maiden Voyage Begins

1. Titanic: *Futility* by Morgan Robertson. **http://www.historyon thenet.com/Titanic/futility.htm**

2. Ibid.

Chapter 3 The Fateful Day

1. Walter Lord, *The Night Lives On* (New York: William Morrow and Company, 1986), p. 65.

2. David G. Brown, *The Last Log of the* Titanic (New York: McGraw Hill, 2001), p. 28.

3. Don Lynch, Titanic: *An Illustrated History* (New York: Hyperion, 1992), p. 83.

4. Ibid.

Chapter 4 "Iceberg Right Ahead"

1. Walter Lord, *A Night to Remember: Illustrated Edition* (New York: Holt, Rinehart and Winston, 1976), p. 33.

2. Robert D. Ballard with Michael S. Sweeney, *Return to* Titanic: *A New Look at the World's Most Famous Lost Ship* (Washington, D.C.: National Geographic, 2004), p. 29.

3. Lawrence Beesley, *The Loss of the S.S.* Titanic: *Its Story and Its Lessons* (Boston: Houghton Mifflin, 2000; reprinted from the 1912 edition), p. 55.

4. Robert D. Ballard, *The Discovery of the* Titanic (New York: Madison Publishing Company, 1987), p. 83.

Chapter 5 How Could Such a Horrible Event Happen?

1. Don Lynch, Titanic: *An Illustrated History* (New York: Hyperion, 1992), p. 182.

2. David G. Brown, *The Last Log of the* Titanic (New York: McGraw Hill, 2001), p. 3.

3. Paul Louden-Brown. "Ismay and the *Titanic.*" **http://www.titanic historicalsociety.org/articles/ ismay.asp**

4. Ibid.

5. Ibid.

6. Wyn Craig Wade, *The* Titanic: *End of a Dream* (New York: Penguin Books, 1986), p. 288.

7. Brown, p. 10.

8. Ibid., p. 168.

9. Ibid.

10. Lawrence Beesley, *The Loss of the S.S.* Titanic: *Its Story and Its Lessons* (Boston: Houghton Mifflin, 2000; reprinted from the 1912 edition), p. 160.

11. Ibid., p. 161.

12. Wade, p. 321.

13. Beesley, pp. 161–62.

14. Walter Lord, *The Night Lives On* (New York: William Morrow and Company, 1986), pp. 79–80.

15. Beesley, p. 41.

16. Brown, p. 140.

17. Ibid., p. 147.

Glossary

aft (AFT)
Toward the rear of a boat or ship.

bias (BY-us)
Favoring one side in a debate or argument.

bow (BOW as in DOWN)
The front of a boat or ship.

epitomized (ee-PIH-tuh-mized)
Stood as the highest example or representation of something.

keel (KEEL)
The center portion of the bottom of a ship's hull.

lucrative (LOO-kruh-tiv)
Very profitable.

pneumatic tube (new-MAA-tik toob)
A pipe that uses compressed air to transport objects.

proverb (PRAH-vurb)
A brief statement about a certain situation that appears to be always true.

scapegoat (SKAPE-goht)
A person or group of people who are given primary responsibility for an unfortunate event, allowing others to evade punishment.

stern (STURN)
The rear of a boat or ship.

vulgar (VUL-gur)
Commonplace, ordinary, undistinguished, lacking good taste.

whitewash (WHITE-wash)
To cleanse or cover up dirty details.

Further Reading

For Young Adults

Ballard, Robert D. *Exploring the* Titanic. New York: Scholastic, 1998.

Blos, Joan W. *The Heroine of the* Titanic. New York: Morrow Junior Books, 1991.

Brewster, Hugh. *882 1/2 Amazing Answers to Your Questions About the* Titanic. New York: Scholastic, 1999.

Bunting, Eve. *SOS* Titanic. New York: Harcourt, 1996.

Crisp, Marty. *White Star: A Dog on the* Titanic. New York: Holiday House, 2004.

Marschall, Ken. *Inside the* Titanic: *A Giant Cut-away Book*. New York: Little Brown, 1997.

Osborne, Will, and Mary Pope Osborne. *Magic Tree House® Research Guide:* Titanic. New York: Random House, 2002.

Tanaka, Shelley. *On Board the* Titanic: *What It Was Like When the Great Liner Sank*. New York: Hyperion Books for Children, 1996.

White, Ellen Emerson. *Voyage on the Great* Titanic: *The Diary of Margaret Ann Brady*. New York: Scholastic, 1998.

Works Consulted

Ballard, Robert D. *The Discovery of the* Titanic. New York: Madison Publishing Company, 1987.

Ballard, Robert D., with Michael S. Sweeney. *Return to* Titanic: *A New Look at the World's Most Famous Lost Ship*. Washington, D.C.: National Geographic, 2004.

Beesley, Lawrence. *The Loss of the S.S.* Titanic: *Its Story and Its Lessons*. Boston: Houghton Mifflin, 2000; reprinted from the 1912 edition.

Brown, David G. *The Last Log of the* Titanic. New York: McGraw Hill, 2001.

Lord, Walter. *The Night Lives On*. New York: William Morrow and Company, 1986.

————. *A Night to Remember: Illustrated Edition*. New York: Holt, Rinehart and Winston, 1976.

Lynch, Don. Titanic: *An Illustrated History*. New York: Hyperion, 1992.

McCluskie, Tom, Michael Sharpe, and Leo Marriott. Titanic *and Her Sisters* Olympic *and* Britannic. San Diego, CA: Thunder Bay Press, 1998.

Wade, Wyn Craig. *The* Titanic: *End of a Dream*. New York: Penguin Books, 1986.

On the Internet

Dr. Robert Ballard
http://www.titanic-titanic.com/robert_ballard.shtml

The Great Ocean Liners: "Ship Histories"
http://www.greatoceanliners.net/index2.html

History of the White Star Line and the International Mercantile Marine
http://www.titanic-whitestarships.com/History_WSL.htm

The Molly Brown House Museum
http://mollybrown.org/

The Sinking of *Titanic*
http://www.rmwexplorations.com/theories.htm

The Teacher's Guide: "*Titanic* Timeline"
http://www.theteachersguide.com/Titanictimeline.html

Titanic Historical Society
http://www.titanic1.org/

Titanic Inquiry Project
http://www.titanicinquiry.org/

Titanic: A Special Exhibit from Encyclopedia Britannica
http://search.eb.com/titanic/

Titanic – Futility by Morgan Robertson
http://www.historyonthenet.com/Titanic/futility.htm

Willing, Richard. "Belfast Sees Hope for Unity in Titanic Project." *USA Today*, May 27, 2005.
http://www.keepmedia.com/pubs/USATODAY/2005/05/27/871168?extID=10026

Wood, Captain Eric D. *Damage to Titanic: A New Scenario*.
http://home.comcast.net/~bwormst7/Symposium/ErikWood.doc

Index